UNBROKEN, UNBENT, UNBOWED

Unbroken, Unbent, Unbowed

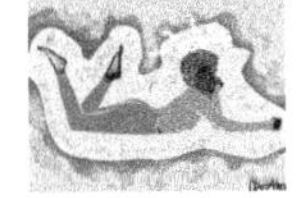

Contents

DJELI JOURNAL

UnBroken
Unbent
Unbowed
ISSUE 1 - March 2026
A Publication of Stories, Memory, and Creative Resistance
Edited by Desiree McCray and Kyron Elam

LETTER FROM THE EDITOR

Dearest Reader,

I extend a warm embrace and my most sincere and heartfelt gratitude for your joining us on this monumental journey with DJELI JOURNAL. As the esteemed Editor-in-Chief, I feel honored to usher you into the inaugural issue of this aesthetic and literary endeavor, a space where justice, resilience, and the power of storytelling coalesce to stitch together a vibrant quilt of otherwise dismissed narratives.

DJELI JOURNAL represents more than just words jumping off the page; it marks the amplification of a kaleidoscope of visionary voices that have often been marginalized or overlooked in the mainstream literary landscape. I started DJELI because I've been in rooms where our brilliance was underestimated, our voices sidelined, our words tone-policed, and our truth deemed inconvenient or "too much." I started DJELI because gatekeeping in publishing is real—and I got tired of asking for permission to be seen, heard, and valued on the page.

DJELI (pronounced jelly) goes beyond publishing; it's a home where stories endure. A haven where diversity is not only included but celebrated. A literary sanctuary for radical truth-tellers, cultural keepers, and prophetic poets. It's the platform I needed when I was a younger writer—hungry to speak, but unsure where my voice fit in a world that often tried to erase it. Thus, DJELI is rooted in legacy. In testimony. In the belief that our stories are sacred, our poems are powerful, and our literature is necessary for liberation.

We're here to break open space.

We exist to nurture work that remembers the ancestors and dreams up a freer future.

At the heart of our mission is the transmutation of oral histories into written archives. In West African tradition, the djeli—oral storytellers, and gatekeepers of histories—held a sacred role in preserving and disseminating the narratives of their ancestries and communities. Drawing wisdom and inspiration from this thousand-year-old tradition, we cherish that storytelling embodies a timeless conduit that transcends time, locations, and generations. DJELI JOURNAL strives to affirm this tradition while echoing a modern twist of preserving narratives for generations to come.

In these pages you will witness women reclaim agency, trans people break barriers, and women erect boundaries. Women who refuse to bow. Women who tell unshakeable truths. Threads of defiance and self-definition led us to our theme: *Unbroken, Unbent, Unbowed.* The contributors help us to reimagine what it means to need and to become our own Black superheroes. They name the courage required to close the door on those who seek our bodies without extending intention or care. They honor Black women's indomitable spirit.

The voices that grace these pages constitute the DNA of DJELI JOURNAL. This collection of stories, essays, and poems, help us to grow in the knowledge of Sankofa—the Ghanaian principle that means "go back and fetch it." To the Akan tribe in Ghana, the Sankofa bird is symbolized by a bird's body facing forward while its head looks back. This ancestral wisdom recounts that by learning from the past we can ensure a strong future. We must know where we come from, to know where we are going. Sankofa embodies the reason why we champion oral history's transmutation and why we bear witness to the divine responsibility to be truth-tellers and truth-seekers.

The West African djeli worked not only as griots but as bearers of a sacred duty to safeguard the histories of their people. Even as diasporans, displaced from our homeland and dispersed across the globe, we refuse to abandon this venerated tradition.

We acknowledge that displacement cannot erase our creative accounts of history or disrupt the relevance of our cultural inheritance; instead, it furnishes an opportunity to intertwine narratives that transcend borders and connect us all. DJELI JOURNAL serves as a testament to the enduring legacy of storytelling, regardless of geographical boundaries. I'm proud to note that we received submissions from across the Diaspora located in Africa, the Caribbean islands, the United States, and Europe.

Because you, dear reader, have decided to spend time within these blest pages, I extend my whole-hearted appreciation. Thank you for being part of this movement to uplift, remember, laud, and preserve the narratives that make us distinctively human. As we embark on this journey together, let us celebrate the power of literature to foster understanding, vulnerability, empathy, and unity. In the spirit of the djeli, let our stories rise among us, resonating across the time and space continuum, and leaving an indelible mark on the pages of history. This work reveals itself as a vessel propelling the voices of the past into a bright, illustrious future.

Yours in the Movement,
Desiree McCray, Editor-in-Chief
DJELI JOURNAL

What We Need

G inger M. Galloway (she/her) writes (and illustrates) children's fiction, novellas, and poetry. She enjoys exploring any variety of genres. She holds her BA in Human Development from Azusa Pacific University. Her published credits include "Gerald Learned to Tie His Shoes" (AG Publishing, 2020), "Cholla Needles" literary magazine (Chollaneedles.com, issues 86, 88 and 104), "These Black Bodies" anthology (Inlandia Institute, 2023), "On Being a Teacher and Other Questionable Decisions" (Jamii Publishing, 2023). Ginger is the co-founder of Wild Seed Poetry and Arts Collective (wildseedpad.org) and editor of the Wild Seed PAC anthology, "Saltwater" (Jamii Publishing, 2024).

What We Need

A POEM by Ginger M. Galloway

we need a BLACK SUPERHERO
to FLY in with the wind to SAVE the DAY
a BLACK SUPERHERO wearing
an AFRO and GOLD rimmed
SHADES
he ought to have SWAG and DRIP
his THEME MUSIC being something
with a little JAZZ and a little HIP HOP
AND a little FUNK
you say we already had MARCUS and
MALCOM and BARACK and KAMALA
COREY and SHIRLEY
and 'nem AUNTIES and 'nem UNCLES
but we need one who can LEAP tall buildings

and to be STRONGER than bullets
you say we had T'chala and Shuri and
CYBORG, LUKE CAGE, MILES MORALES
BUMBLEBEE
BUT we need a REAL live
BLACK SUPERHERO
for these real live VILLAINS
a HERO
who won't put up with the BULLSHIT
of flags and patriots
it's all a LIE anyway
he will come with TRUTH and HONOR
for all things like HIM
he'll be the BLACK HIRE and do
a DAMN GOOD BLACK JOB
he will DESTROY the past with
HOPE and PROMISE for TOMORROW
and we will know that he FIGHTS FOR
US
and we won't call him THAT
we won't call him OUR SUPERHERO
we will instead
give him a nickname like
JUNEBUG or ROSCOE
or SHUG
or TYRONE
and we will feel SAFE
like every POLLYANNA they told us
needed SAVING

The Other 37 Cents

Tishayla J. Williams is a doctoral candidate in Business Administration at Capella University, an I/O psychologist, social scientist, and U.S. Army veteran. She serves as the founder of The TW Collective, LLC, a consulting firm specializing in corporate compliance, accountability, and strategic transformation across all levels of leadership. Her independent research examines pay equity for Black women and the advancement of workplace rights for all. Her forthcoming book explores equity and economic justice for Black women in corporate America. Guided by the principles of Impact. Equity. Strategy., Tishayla's work is rooted in building a fairer world for the next generation.

The Other 37 Cents

AN ESSAY by Tishayla J. Williams

I used to think the difference was just numbers.

Thirty-seven cents. That's what separates me from the full dollar. The average Black woman makes 63 cents for every dollar a white man earns. I've read the reports. I've cited the statistics. But no chart or graph prepares you for what that gap feels like.

Thirty-seven cents is quiet theft. It's the unpaid hours I've spent reviewing someone else's resume. It's the after-work phone call from a friend who needs help with rent. It's every moment I gave more than I had because "you're doing better than most."

The truth? I was doing better than I had been. But not by much. And certainly not enough to shoulder the quiet expectations that came with simply appearing to keep them together.

I didn't make it. I joined. I went to all the schools. Got all the degrees. Did all the right things. And I still struggled. Still do. Just in different zip codes, with fancier problems and better vocabulary to explain them.

I come from women who did what they had to do.

My mother was a stay-at-home mom for most of my childhood. But when her marriage began to crack, she knew she couldn't rely on anyone else to hold her future. She enrolled in classes to become a legal assistant. I remember being in classrooms with her, notebooks in her lap, children at her feet. We don't talk much now, but I still carry the imprint of those moments—watching a woman try to build something steady in the middle of instability.

My maternal grandmother worked when she was allowed. Her husband controlled the household, and her independence came in small, hard-earned pieces. Odd jobs, whispered paychecks, work that didn't ask too many questions. She survived by shrinking herself and stretching every dollar.

And my paternal grandmother, out, proud, and unapologetic, worked security her entire life. She held her ground in uniforms, in workplaces, and in her identity. She didn't flinch. She didn't bend. She was proof that you could be firm and free simultaneously.

These women didn't get to rest. They didn't get the luxury of soft choices or second chances. And even if I don't carry all their closeness, I carry their grit. Their instinct. Their need to prepare for the moment when the world stops protecting you and starts asking how you'll survive.

The wage gap isn't just about earnings. It's about erosion.

Our health suffers when high co-pays keep us from attending therapy, or when we stretch our medication to last until payday. Relationships are strained by exhaustion that prevents us from being fully engaged or compassionate. The future becomes uncertain when we give all our energy to others without investing in our own financial security, rest, or aspirations.

I've had jobs where I was praised publicly but paid quietly. Where white men I trained made more than I did. Where "diversity" was a photo on the company website but not a commitment in policy.

You learn to internalize the lack, stretch, smile, and give 100% for a 63% return.

And then they call you resilient.

What people call resilience; I now recognize as residue.

The residue of being the strong one. The go-to. The backup plan and the foundation.

Many individuals have experienced aiding others while making personal sacrifices. I recall a particular week when I chose to pay another person's overdue phone bill at the expense of my own grocery shopping, without disclosing this decision to anyone. At that time, I was employed full-time. On paper, I was "stable." But behind closed doors, I was playing financial Tetris just to survive.

That's the thing about being a Black woman who looks like she has it all together: people assume you do. They don't see the sleepless nights. The loans are in deferment. The jobs you stay in because leaving means losing health insurance. They just see the smile. The LinkedIn post. The degrees.

When you finally refuse or step away, they gaze at you as though you've let them down.

The wage gap steals more than money.

It steals softness. It steals time. It steals the opportunity to just... be.

Because while others are figuring out what brings them joy, we're figuring out how to cover the light bill. While they take sabbaticals, we're taking care of parents, siblings, children—not because we're martyrs, but because there's no one else.

We are our own safety net. And we're tired.

I don't want applause for surviving. I want to change.

I want workplaces to stop using our labor and ignoring our voices. I want policies that don't just close pay gaps but open doors. I want care work to be paid, not praised and forgotten. I want to see a world where Black women's value isn't discounted at every register—literal and metaphorical.

And until that world exists, I'm reclaiming my 37 cents.

That means saying no when I'm depleted. That means investing in my healing, even when others say it's selfish. That means recognizing that strength without support is a setup.

I still show up for people—but now, I also show up for myself.

This isn't just my experience; many have acted strong while carrying their burdens.

You know if you've ever had to stretch one paycheck over ten needs. You know it if you've ever been told to "be grateful" for crumbs. You know if you've ever been to both the success story and the emergency contact.

We were never meant to do this alone. But we were taught too. Conditioned too. I was applauded for it.

So, here's my offer: the truth.

The wage gap is a significant and persistent issue. It stems from systemic, personal, and historical factors. It is important that we acknowledge its existence and stop treating it as an accepted norm.

Because we deserve full dollars. Full lives. And full rest. Not just what's left over after everyone else eats.

We begin by insisting on transparency in salaries, promotions, and hiring. We push for policies that protect caregivers and compensate for emotional labor. We support Black women-owned businesses, donate to mutual aid funds, and show up when it's not convenient. We stop telling Black women they are strong and start asking them what they need both personally and professionally. It begins when we as Black women create boundaries with family, friends, and coworkers.

We don't need saviors. We need support. We need allies who listen before they lead, and systems that work without needing to be burned down first.

Progress won't come from a single solution. But it will come when enough people decide that 63% effort for 100% excellence is no longer acceptable.

Transformation is achieved when we collectively ensure that change becomes inevitable.

At the time of this writing, I am one of 350,000 Black women who were either let go or chose to step down from their positions in March 2025. This transition is not a retreat, but a strategic move that reflects broader economic shifts: as of August 2025, Black women are the most educated demographic and the fastest-growing group of entrepreneurs in the United States, BUT WE HAVE THE HIGHEST UNEMPLOYMENT RATE.

I transitioned from my previous position to establish TW Collective, a consulting firm dedicated to advocating for individuals with particular emphasis on supporting Black women and promoting corporate accountability. I begin this next phase of my life on my own terms—armed with two and a half degrees, a bit of savings, and no traditional safety net of a husband or parental support. The time for settling for 63 cents is over. I CAN'T SIT BY. I am building a future that requires the white man's full dollar.

Sixteen Inches Lighter

J**alyn Lankford** (she/her) is a writer and human services professional whose work frequently explores themes of queerness, identity, liberation, and cultural shifts. Her essay, "Sixteen Inches Lighter," is a personal account of her decision to cut her hair —a symbolic act of defiance against the pressures of beauty standards and the concept of "pretty privilege." Through this transformation, she reclaims her self-worth and encourages readers to embrace their authentic selves, regardless of external acceptance. To read more from Jalyn, you can find her work as a Contributor to the magazine, *The 20-Something Files*, online, under the pen name Lyny.

Sixteen Inches Lighter

A PERSONAL REFLECTION by Jalyn Lankford

I knew my grandma would lovingly mention my hair again when it grew out. It suddenly became a taboo topic during my bob days. She would still complement me when I had cute clips or a bow in, but I know she secretly hoped no scissors would ever come near me, not even to cut split ends.

I knew my aunt would play in my hair again, gently grazing my forehead as she braided each strand. When my mom announced to the family that I was getting the big chop, she suggested I try a wig out first. She relented, but to her, long hair is more feminine.

Hair holds deep value in my family and for many Black families. Having "good hair" that is "manageable" is what so many Black women are told to strive for, and why we often put these pressures on each other. Each strand represents our history, our courage, our privilege, and our perceived beauty in the world. For me, though, it represented a façade I couldn't wait to cut off. Sixteen inches would do just fine.

I grew up going to my grandparents' church every Sunday. In the Black church, everyone is family, and the grandchildren of the Bishop and First Lady receive extra attention. Not to mention, my sister, cousin, and I were the only girls out of ten grandchildren, so we had different expectations of how to act in our matching dresses and little tights. How I would have gladly gotten messy for a chance to have fun. I looked pretty and polite with my long hair. The church ladies ran their fingers through my hair while having grown-up conversations. I never minded—I enjoy head massages, but that was *all* I was known for. Even strangers would approach me and ask if they could have my hair. I was their Barbie, and for a time, I was happy to be. I enjoyed the attention, but it never went deeper. My appearance superseded my intelligence and passions.

It came to a point where I lay on my mother's bed, confused and estranged from my emotions. The game show channel was on, but even a horror movie would not snap me out of my funk. What was wrong with me? As I evaluated my body for insecurities, I reached my head and realized the root of my hatred. My curls were choking me, and I wanted out. That night, I took the biggest leap of faith and decided to go for the big chop.

Several thoughts ran through my mind, most of which mean nothing to me now. Still, the one that pushed me to move the most was the fear that guys would no longer like me. My extensive research, which began and finished on Quora, proved that men find women with longer hair more beautiful, classy, and acceptable for marriage. What would I be without a man's praise? Well, I am happily a lesbian, but those cringey ideals were my lifeline back then: to be accepted and desired. I was afraid of being perceived differently and labeled— I only wanted to be regarded with the same care as my male counterparts. In internalizing these feelings, I othered myself and became my biggest enemy. My family would miss my hair, but they love me regardless and would get over it. Who cares what a man thinks, anyway? So it was up to me to determine if *I* could let this go and take a chance on something authentic.

I sat in the salon, unafraid and ready. When the first section was cut, a literal and spiritual weight fell to the ground. I was free and never felt happier. I have reclaimed my hair and confidence. Beauty is in the eye of the beholder, but most importantly, it is in the eye of the wearer.

Samson & Delilah

Jo JB Schaffer (they/he/she) lives as an interdisciplinary writer and performing artist, working in music, theatre, and film. Jo's work regularly explores stories about identity and the ways experience often impacts one's identity. Jo engages in many works in progress, with music published under Top Pop Productions, their independent music production company and music publisher. You can find their music on all streaming platforms under "joJB" and "The Tapestries Collective." You can find Jo's art and culture articles for Scapi Magazine at ScapiMag.com.

Samson & Delilah

A PLAY by Jo J.B. Schaffer

Characters: SKIP, MARTHA
Props/Furniture: a bench, a swaddled baby, a bus stop (optional)

[SKIP enters with his son swaddled. As soon as he steps into the playing space it's feeding time.]
SAMSON: Whaaaa whaaa whaaaaaaa
SKIP: Okay, okay
(Skip finds the only seat on stage, preferably a bench.)
(Skip prepares.)
SAMSON: Whaaa whaaa
SKIP: Okay!
(Skip lifts his shirt over one shoulder and allows Samson to latch.)
SAMSON: (Coos.)
SKIP: There! See? Daddy would never let his little man go hungry now would he?
MARTHA: (Entering on the phone. She has a non midwestern accent that could be from anywhere, the actor's best, directors best discretion.)
And so then I walked by her office and saw her shaving her legs! I know! Shaving her legs, I'm like what the hell? All pathos out the window, first week and she's already on my--
(Sees Skip and Samson.)
Oh my GOD! Maribel I have to go!
(To Skip.)
Sir! Sir! What ever are you doing with that baby?
SKIP: (A moment.) I'm feeding him. The fuck does it look like?
MARTHA: You're... oh.. but you're... OH! You can still do that?
SKIP: (A moment.) Yes.
MARTHA: Oh, I didn't know that....
(She stares.)
SKIP: Bus stop's down there, Miss.
MARTHA: The father..
SKIP: Yes, me?

MARTHA: You mean there's not another father?

SKIP: He was made by a man and a woman.

MARTHA: So your wife--

SKIP: Partner.

MARTHA: Your.. partner... is she also...

SKIP: Trans? Yes.. (brief silence.) What's your gender?

MARTHA: Oh I'm a female.

SKIP: I see... well miss...?

MARTHA: Martha.

SKIP: Miss Martha. Show's over.

(Skip puts his shirt back down.)

MARTHA: Oh, I'm... I'm sorry. I didn't mean to stare. It's just that I've never met a transgender before.

SKIP: Trans person.

MARTHA: Transperson... Can I, can I see him?

SKIP: (Thinks. Looks to Samson.)

Samsie, you wanna go to the crazy lady?

(Looks back to Martha.)

Maybe for a moment.

MARTHA: Oh, thank you!

(Martha takes Samson in her arms.)

He's, he's beautiful. His name's Samsie?

SKIP: Samson.

MARTHA: Samson.. and your name?

SKIP: Skip.

MARTHA: Skip. It's very nice to meet you and.. Samson.. both very handsome young men.

SKIP: Why, thank you.

MARTHA: I wish you could meet my niece Delilah. She's his age. You know it's good to socialize them with children their age as soon as possible.

SKIP: He has infant cousins.

MARTHA: Oh good, oh good   Well this has been nice.. And informative.

SKIP: I'm glad.

(Martha hands Samson back to Skip.)

MARTHA: Maybe I'll see you around.

SKIP: See ya around, Martha.

(She exits.)

END PLAY.

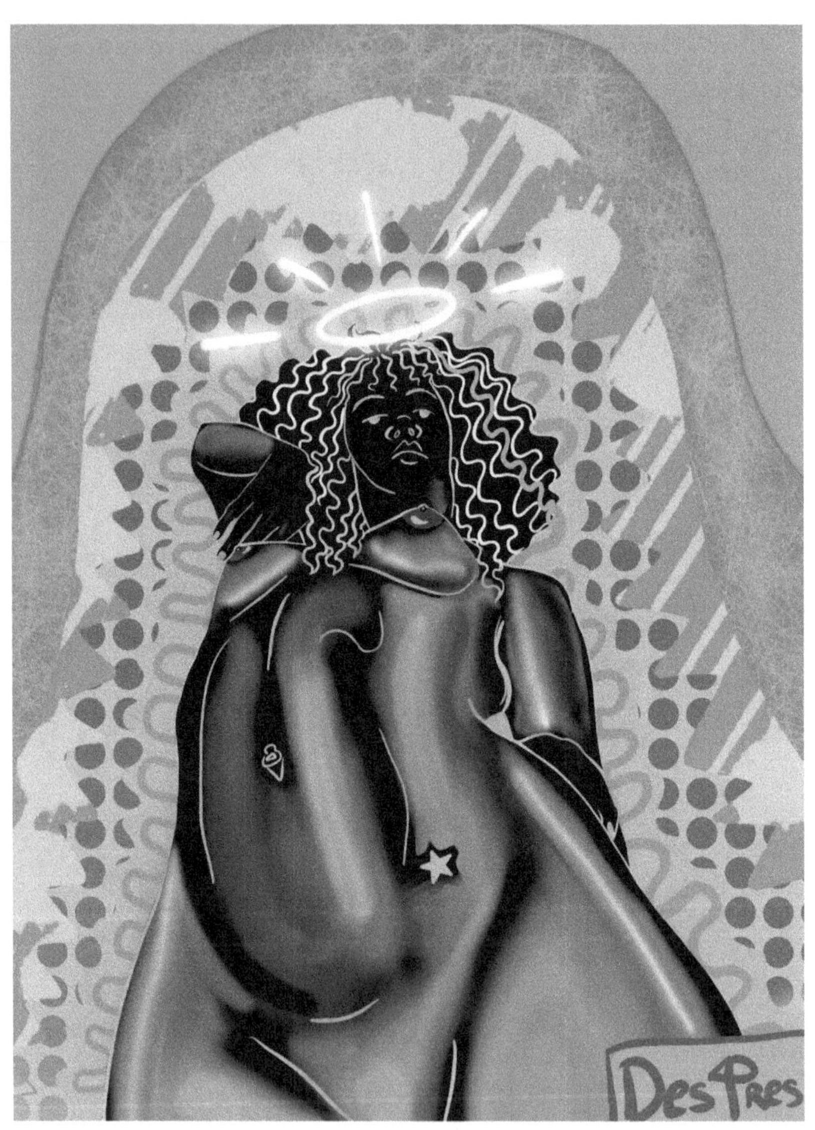
DesPres

I'm Taking Sexy Back

Diana Sanchez (she/her) is a 20 year old faith based aspiring journalist and author from west Florida. Her main works include expansive research essays, think pieces about life, and descriptive poetry. Growing up, she always struggled to say what was on her mind, due to her shyness and sensitivity to other people's feelings, so she took those thoughts and wrote them down. She began publishing her work on Substack in August 2024 under the name "Yap University". She changed her publication name to "xoxo, Diana" in January 2025, introducing a more personal approach to her writing.

I'm Taking Sexy Back

AN ESSAY by Diana Sanchez

Formal Content Warning:

Discussions of Grooming and Sexual Assault. If such content offends you or brings you to a traumatic place, please take care of yourself and exit this essay.

I'm going to be 100% honest. I knew I was sexy before I knew what it meant. What I mean is that I was seen as an object of lust from a very young age. It's a sad thing to come to terms with, especially since I'm still very young, having now been twenty for some months. I've allowed myself to lust and to be lusted after, purely out of wanting to be seen.

My elementary school days are where it all started. I remember being six years old and looking at the way my kindergarten teacher's daughter walks. She had a specific sway in her hips, one that I tried to imitate the first day I saw her. It was that day that I remember my mom telling me very sternly to "stop switching." For those that aren't black or didn't grow up around southern black people, "switching" is a way of saying that I was walking like I was selling my body. Imagine getting told that as an elementary school kid.

Yeah, that'll really do it.

When puberty hit me at nine years old, I truly felt my image change in people's eyes. While everybody was celebrating buy their first training bra in fifth grade, I was already wearing underwire bras at a 34B cup size. I watched as girls my age grew jealous of and boys staring at my bosom in the middle of class. That was my first introduction to groping. Having random 10- and 11-year-old boys trying to grab your chest while you pass them by is so weird, especially when just last year, no one seemed to notice. Now all of a sudden, nipples become a second set of eyes.

Middle school was definitely the time where hormones that I didn't know I had were discovered. It was also the time where I learned that your body is a weapon, and it has nothing to do with your fists. Seeing how I would be made into a villain for simply existing was already weird in elementary school, but in middle school? Oh, my goodness. Seeing friends turn to enemies just because their crush wanted to know what boobs were. Having grown women tell you that your mere existence is a distraction from learning to boys whose voices and ballsacks just dropped a month ago. Having grown men stare at your chest and everyone thinking it's normal and not saying anything because you're just a girl.

High school made it no better. Sex seemed to be everywhere. You couldn't have a conversation with any 14- or 15-year-old boy or girl without the topic of sex being thrown around. Everything got sexualised. The way you sat, the way you talked, even glasses got pornified (yes, I made that up) due to their association with stars like Mia Khalifa. It was these perceptions that led to me being in the hands of men that groomed and sexually assaulted for the first and second time in my life in high school. I began to fear the word "sexy". I tried to avoid it like it was the coronavirus. Unfortunately for me, that was harder done than said, as my last ex-boyfriend seemed to think that word was one of the only adjectives in the dictionary.

Going from being super hypersexual to being more reserved about the word was a very odd shift. To most people's shock, I was a virgin all throughout high school, and even my freshman year of college. I never talked about my sex life because I didn't have one, and even if I did, whoever is making me moan in pleasure is no one's business. It felt as though everyone had this stereotype about pretty women, which is that all of us are these coquetteish whores. It's hard to explain to people that it was never hard for me to resist sex because most of the dudes seemed to have no spiritual foundation, abysmal emotional intelligence, and no understanding that washing between your butt crack doesn't determine your sexuality.

Even when I was in my super hypersexual phase, I never gave names. If you knew, you knew. It was that simple. Most of my friends didn't even know that I had any form of sexual attraction to my past boyfriends until we broke up. I kept it in the closet so much you would think I was purposely trying to live out the Michael Jackson song.

My initial introduction to sex was not a very healthy one. It was preteen and teenaged boys playing porn in school like it was a new Playboi Carti record. I didn't get the sex talk until I was 14 years old, so I genuinely was concerned every time I heard it in the hallway on a BOSE speaker at full volume. It wasn't until my senior year of high school when I got my first true sexual awakening. At least, in a healthy way. Not through physical contact or any stern talking to, but through music.

Janet Jackson and Rauw Alejandro are definitely not people that you think of when you think of people that would be healthy sex educators, but they were for me. I had grown up on Janet and I had been a fan of Rauw since 2020, and both reframed my way of viewing sex. I would go into a whole tangent about them both, but I have already done so in various essays on my personal blog "xoxo, Diana", so I'll spare y'all for now. To put it simply, I now had musical representations of emotional maturity manifesting into sexual intimacy. That sex is more than just going in and out.

Giving my life to Christ also allowed me to change my views on sex and my own image as a sexual being. When you grew up in church like I did, you tend to only hear sex as something that is done within the covenant of marriage. There is also purity culture and the consistent reminder that you as a woman are a sexual distraction that causes every man past the age of 11 to stumble. When 2024 came and I decided to rededicate my life to Jesus, I allowed the Lord to work on the spirit of lust that was in my heart.

It was difficult, truthfully, going from viewing yourself as a hole to a whole person. I was freshly 19, and it seemed like that was the age that everyone said that love was for the birds. Nasty 19 should be in full effect, but it wasn't for me. My experience with working through lust led me to cut out a lot of things out of obedience. Erotica writing, masturbation, certain artists I was listening to, even certain kinds of underwear I owned, but that's a story for another time.

The hardest kind of sexual healing is never physical. It's spiritual.

My way of healing was prayer. I remember it like it was yesterday, sitting in my room trying to get some sleep, but couldn't. I was thinking about too many things, one of which being my sexual assault story. I felt so dirty, wanting to peel my skin off and just cry. I prayed and asked God to take this feeling away. To deliver me from the agony of the belief that I will be sexually dirty for the rest of my life.

I felt a sudden wind blow in my room, whispering "Pure". I was so confused, but also…free? I knew that God was real, right? I knew Jesus was real then. There was no denying it at that point. It was the calmest form of deliverance I've ever known.

I hadn't had a single lustful thought since that day in August. Even after I had a failed talking stage with a guy I met on my way to work, nothing. The enemy would try, but it never prevailed. I was fully convinced that I was just never going to be a married woman because I lacked sexual experience and at the same time, had very little sexual urges. That was until the present day.

March 14 th , 2025 is the day that I said yes to the most amazing man that a young woman could ask for. No, I'm not married yet, but I know in my spirit that he's the one. The strangest feeling about it though, is that I am feeling sexual urges again. I was dreaming about my boyfriend in my room, and at once, I felt my body react through sweat. I'm not going to go into full blown horny details, but it felt so weird. I'm asking God to get me out because I'm naturally assuming that I was lusting after my man in an unhealthy way. Only for the Lord to tell me, "No, you're okay. You're just feeling things for your husband, and that's okay."

The battle between flesh and spirit in terms of sexual desire is hard to fight. No one showed me what healthy sexual desire looked like, especially in Christ. I thought sexual desire was ravenous, a hunger that needed to be satisfied, or like a predator and its prey. However, this dream felt nothing like that. There was no aggressive ripping of clothes, scratches, or any kind of roughness. I was savoured, cherished, and loved. I didn't feel violated, but comforted. I watched myself be pleasured and not played with. Tenderly. And it felt great. So, so great.

I say all of this not to encourage lust before marriage in anyone who may read this essay of mine, but I say it to say that there is freedom. Where the Lord is, there is freedom, even in sex.

Run to it.

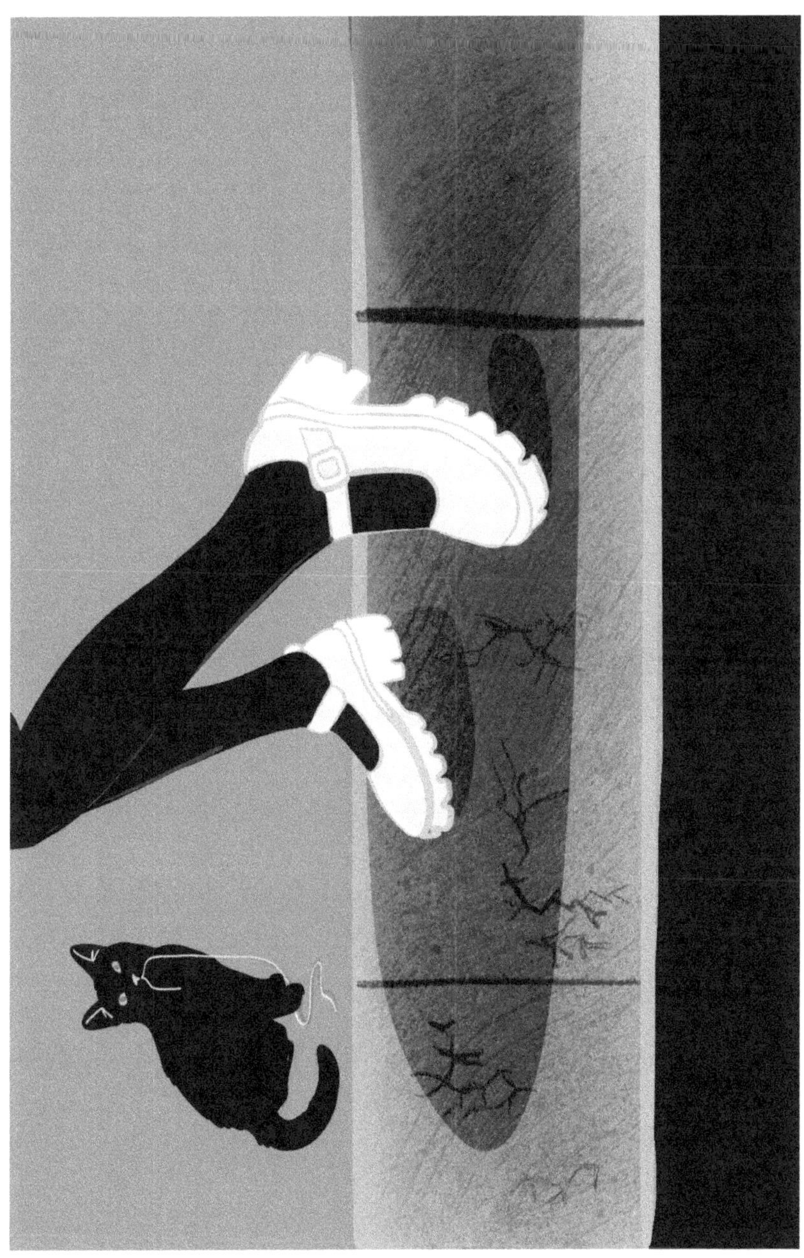

No Pussy for Losers

Franceska Bruny (she/her) is a multidisciplinary artist, writer, and organizer whose work explores the intersections of faith, identity, and liberation. Rooted in her Haitian heritage and shaped by experiences across Boston and Los Angeles, she creates to heal, provoke, and build community. Whether through film, photography, or essays, Franceska uplifts the voices of the marginalized—especially Black and Brown communities—while honoring art as a spiritual practice. An educator, budding philosopher, and current seminary student, she blends intellect with imagination, always guided by the belief that creativity is a divine call. Her work invites reflection, resistance, and radical hope.

No Pussy for Losers

AN ESSAY by Franceska Bruny

As night fell, I slipped into a ritual I've returned to many times. Dimmed lights. Lavender mist curling through the air from my diffuser, softening every edge of the room. I cued up my sultry playlist—the one marked only with a single rose emoji—and let

Jesse Boykins III croon me into ease. The bass was low, the melodies warm, and I could feel myself sinking deeper into the quiet of it all.

I slid into bed, skin humming, reaching over to my nightstand for what's been keeping me company most nights lately. Fingers grazing the familiar shape, I pulled it close—bell hooks' *Communion.*

Curled up with questions about love and freedom, I asked myself, quietly: lying here alone, no body to hold, no hands to explore—was this what liberation really looked like? Did choosing myself in an empty apartment still carry the intimacy I craved?

From the speaker, as if answering me, Jesse cut through the stillness:

"No Pussy For Losers, cuz beggars can't be choosers"

I ain't had sex in about fifty-leven days and upteen hours, and honestly, it's one of the best things I've done for myself. Abstinence, (not celibacy because I desire marriage and this word be tearing yall asses up), was a choice that didn't initially come from some grand vow or purity crusade. At first, it was a necessity—my body was dealing with PCOS, and sex just wasn't an option. But when the physical stuff began to settle, I didn't immediately go back because my view of my body had shifted. I began to understand that my body was something sacred, with its own demands, its own needs, its own memories, and its own traumas.

Working through these things to eventually rush back to sex, I was met with resistance and intense reactions. While my mind was telling me "yes," my body was for sure telling me "no." Examining my reactions, it became apparent that I didn't miss the act. That my body was in need of a break because something needed my attention, bringing me to question my ideas around sexual freedom. How could I label myself as sexually free if my body wasn't letting me do what I wanted?

Instead of dismissing the nudges of my body, I followed—and where it led me were revelations damn near equivalent to post-nut clarity.

Abstinence taught me to be the liberated woman our ancestor bell hooks speaks of—the kind who doesn't fall in love, but chooses it. Exercising that agency set me free from the endless cycle of falling into lust, cosplaying as love.

"No Love for the Lazy"

My new disposition brought new terms to the table—starting with no longer assuming that a nigga would become the man of my dreams if I just offered a blueprint.

I started to notice that in the midst of situationships and talking phases, most of the time spent outside of hunching was me crafting and handing out blueprints to men who didn't even want to build anything that would sustain. Men who entered my ecosystem, disrupted the flow, and acted like what they were offering was groundbreaking, when really, it was basic at best, and oppressive at worst.

This new clarity reminded me: I'm not here to supervise a man's evolution or manage his becoming while mine gets sidelined. Furthermore, I'm not a sock, cum rag, or the space on the floor he ejaculates onto after three minutes of hard work. The right man won't need to be built from scratch. He'll come with his own blueprint—one he's actually studied—and together, we'll integrate our visions.

As I began to understand this as true, I had to accept that these types of partners kept showing up as mirrors. They reflected the reality that the people I was choosing didn't care to build, because I didn't either.

I've had more than my fair share of situationships, and in most of them, sex was the thread holding things together. It wasn't intimacy, it wasn't curiosity—it was access. Physical access mistaken for emotional depth. And when sex was taken off the table, everything started to crumble. Because without it, there was nothing left to stand on.

These experiences taught me that I was no longer okay being someone who was reduced to skin and orgasms. I am a full person. A galaxy. I carry history, softness, rage, joy, and vision. But so many of the connections I was entertaining couldn't hold that. They didn't even try, nor did they want to.

I started to get irritated by how easy it was to mess with someone and call it something meaningful—a complete misnomer. Some of them were even emotionally open, but it was usually one-sided, leaving me to be the one showing up emotionally. And when I asked for the same in return, their reactions made commitment and reciprocity seem complicated, like I was asking for too much. It left me void of the opportunity to find out what it actually means to build something real.

Sex had officially become boring. As I grew more aware and reflected more on sex—its intricacies, my relationship to it, the traumas I had tangled up in it—I started to realize it was also one of the most common forms of escapism. Similar to so many other vices, it was just another dopamine hit. No pun intended. But I wasn't interested in escaping anymore. Not from my reality, and definitely not in helping someone else escape theirs. I could no longer afford to ignore the signals from my body. I was done with the subtle ways I'd been depriving myself of love. I wanted to break free from every form of self-harm, and continuing to have sex in these ways was doing exactly that. That became even clearer when I started encountering men who valued connection, took their time, and weren't pressed about sex. Some of them knew where I stood and didn't treat it like a threat or a challenge, showing me how attractive self-control and discernment could be.

Eventually, I got to the point where advances of sex didn't offend me anymore. They just saddened me. It made me feel like people had nothing more to offer than dick. As if that was supposed to move me. As if that was supposed to excite me. It revealed to me how disconnected people were and how much people truly avoided being seen in ways that go beyond the physical.

Each offer or pass was the equivalent of someone throwing a bag of chips at me, calling it Sunday dinner, and telling me, "Make it enough." What was I supposed to do with that? Starve?

With every watered down, weak ass loveless offer of sexual exchange I fought back with a mighty blow that confused some and bruised the ego of others,

"No."

"Out Here Actin' Crazy"

The reactions to saying "no" in some instances felt like waging a war. That with each "No," I was somehow doing the most disrespectful thing one can do, having agency.

I believe these reactions come from a few different places. First, I believe it's because of the view and socialization of sex in the Western context. When someone chooses to disengage from it in any form, there's a reaction that views them as pretentious or incapable of participating. I've had many encounters where people assume that I'm stuck up, using my abstinence as a way to "hook a man," or simply that my efforts to deconstruct my thoughts and engagement with sex are extra and a result of me overthinking. So be it, bookie. It goes without saying that abstinence—and sometimes even virginity—is treated like a disease or a nuisance because it removes a form of access that too many people are seeking without offering anything meaningful in return, thus becoming an inconvenience.

Next, I believe part of that reaction comes from how people have internalized what sexual freedom is supposed to look like. While I haven't experienced this directly, I've indirectly heard people discuss sexual freedom and either not include abstinence or simply disregard it altogether. There's room for sexual expression that includes things like orgies, open relationships (which aren't always just about sex), and fluid exploration—but there's rarely space for abstinence to be seen as a valid form of sexual freedom. As liberation.

Lastly, it's apparent that the deeper issue is really about people not knowing how to handle being told "no." The idea of a slow burn can be jarring in a time where everything is built around instant gratification. And let's be forreal—if someone just wants to hit, they can play the long game, kick it, and wait around until they eventually get what they want. Which only proves my point. No is no.

For me, "No" has become a spiritual practice, especially where my body is concerned. Each "no" has given me the chance to be clearer about what I will and won't stand for. It's a boundary. A declaration. Not a rejection, but a redirection toward the love I deserve and desire to participate in. It's not just about withholding—it's about alignment. I'm not responsible for a bruised ego. I'm responsible for honoring myself. And if you can't handle that? That's not my business.

My "no" is an act of resistance, directly attacking the transactional love that we've normalized. A bold repentance from a conditioning that confuses access with intimacy, performance with presence, and bodies with belonging. It's my way of making atonement for all the times I wanted to say no but didn't. For the moments I couldn't. And for the seasons when no one even thought to ask.

"So Let Me Tell You How the Story Goes.."

Fucking with losers left me depleted, physically ill, bored, and far away from love. They are indeed the biggest cowards for awakening the love of a woman without the intention of loving her, as Bob Marley said.

And baby, make no mistake, losers come in all shapes, sizes, gender expressions, and sexual orientations. It's a loser epidemic out here y'all. Be sure to stay safe.

The moment I stopped dealing with these lames, my light came back. I realized I'd made a habit of shrinking myself, dimming my needs to pour into situations that didn't meet me mentally, emotionally, or spiritually. I was finally forced to face the reality of the life I was living: negotiating for love, attention, and presence. And it made me sit with the real question—what do I actually want?

I know now that I want a Sunday dinner kind of love—the slow-cooked, seasoned, nourishing kind. A spread that has enough to share and leaves leftovers for the week. The kind that helps in the kitchen, sets the table, brings dessert or wine, and sits and talks for hours. The kind that builds a bond. The kind that sees me fully clothed with my hairscarf on, unfiltered, and still chooses me.

A love that doesn't call me to compromise for a man—partner, whoever, who isn't committed to growing with me, loving me actively, and respecting me enough to see me as a whole human being. With agency. With power. With a heart that deserves to be held, not handled.

I demand space to continue to practice liberation in many forms. The one that isn't always loud or performative. Liberation from a loveless life. Liberation from silently mourning brokenness. I'm not here to tell you to be abstinent—you're grown and gonna do what you please. But I am going to respectfully say: some of y'all have broken pussies, bussies, and "johnsons" (cue Broken Pussy from Insecure) that need rest, not revolution. Broken by harm, by trauma, by disappointment. And if no one else will say it, I will—you can't fuck your way out of trauma.

It's okay to admit the exhaustion of being desired for your body while your soul starves. The weariness that comes from avoiding rest, reclamation, and healing. That ache? That's your soul calling you into a new love practice. Don't do to yourself what them losers did to you.

I don't know about you, but I know my sexual energy wasn't just meant for performance or release. It's creative. It's sacred. It's revolutionary. It has the power to build worlds, not just break beds. And as I've stopped pouring it into people who couldn't hold me, I began to see myself more clearly and learned to hold myself, shifting my cravings from flesh to depth. From friction to resonance.

As Jesse's song came to a close and the strum of the guitar faded into the air, I found myself circling back to the question that first drifted me into thought. Lying here alone, no body to hold, no hands to explore—was this what liberation really looked like?

Yes.

Even alone, even in the quiet—this is intimacy. This is liberation. The choice to be with myself fully. To slow down. To let the lavender linger, to let the silence speak, to let desire stretch without rushing to fill it.

Yes, choosing myself in this empty apartment still carries the intimacy I crave, because I've stopped waiting for someone else to make me feel held. I've become the one who lights the candles, who draws the bath, who whispers love into my own skin. And that... that is sacred.

Because abstinence is not deprivation—it's devotion.

To myself. To my healing. To the love that is here, to the love I'm cultivating, and the love that's coming.

So on soft and quiet nights when the house is still and I return to my ritual, knowing that I will romance my own skin. Candles lit by the bath tub are not for company, but for communion—with myself, with God, with stillness. Learning how to hold my own hand, how to soothe my own ache, how to sit with desire without letting it drive me.

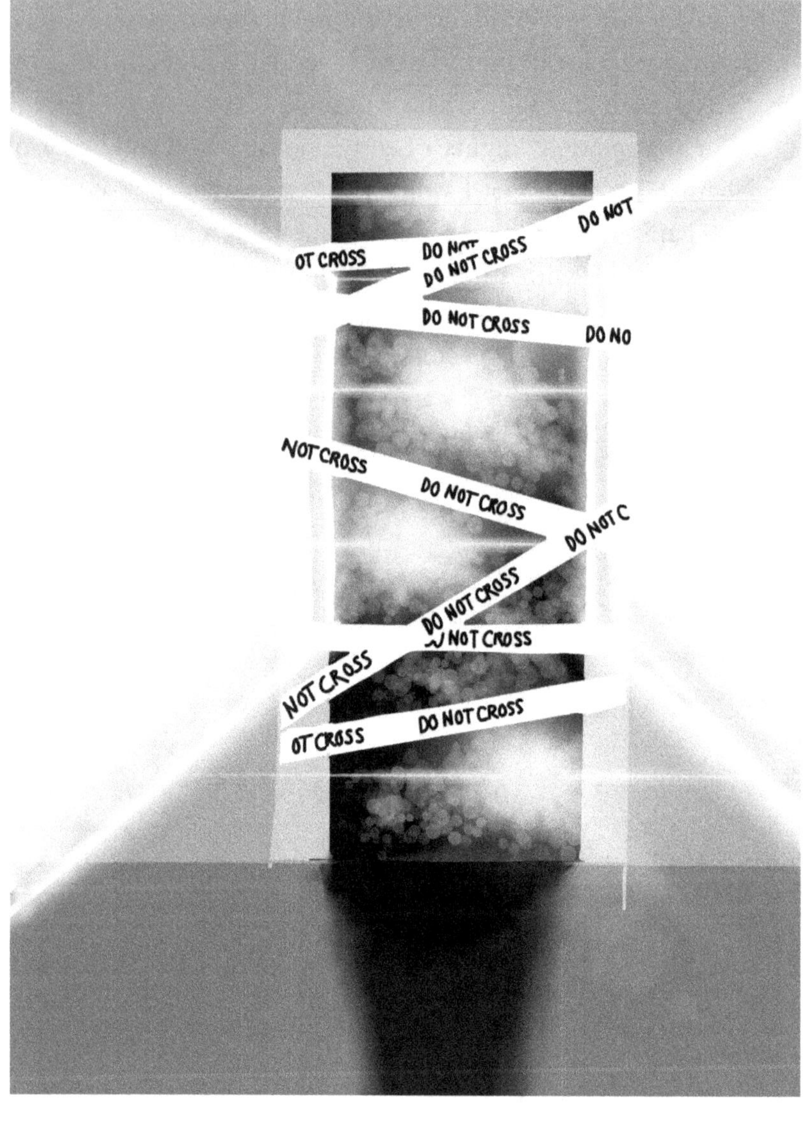
DO NOT
OT CROSS
DO NOT
DO NOT CROSS
DO NOT CROSS
DO NO
NOT CROSS
DO NOT CROSS
DO NOT C
DO NOT CROSS
NOT CROSS
NOT CROSS
OT CROSS
DO NOT CROSS
DO NOT

Dear Black Girls

Jaeda Garner (she/her) is a recent graduate of Grambling State University. A writer of 16 years, Jaeda enjoys writing poetry, plays, and short stories. Her work centers around her experience as a southern, Afro-Panamanian, geeky black girl. Through her works she hopes to create changemaking conversations. She is also a member of Delta Sigma Theta Sorority, Inc. and hopes to leverage her membership to increase visibility in the arts. Her most recent published work is "Recount", a play detailing the journey of a domestic violence survivor, that was recently performed in a reading at the Dallas Academy of Arts and Letters.

Dear Black Girls

A POEM by Jaeda Garner

While you were in the womb something magical happened.
God stitched lace bronze with flecks of gold into your eyes,
He took the essence of a Lion and put it into your soul so you
could see beyond the lies.
The lies they tell you as you grow up.

That you're not pretty enough.
That you're not smart enough.
That you're not enough.
They push you down like roots of a tree into a soil of self-ha-
tred and self-disgust
til you believe that you are just not right
for this world,
so you try to fit into this clam shell idea like a pearl.
You press and press and comb out those curls
but honey that was a god given gift for you
a black girl.
Hair so strong it could stand the test of all elements.
Nose so wide that we can smell the roses from inside.
Hips so large that they can withhold all emotions and carry love
like a barge.
Lips so big that they remind you of a blooming rose
when we open that mouth and speak up we grow.
A black girl
whose arms could go through so much pain yet continue to
push out power
again and again.
Whose legs can withhold hatred, racism, colorism, ignorance,
bigotry but still stand strong and
protest against all hostility
Like I said something magical in the womb happened.
God placed brilliance, creativity and care into your brain to
prepare you
for your journey against the grain

Empty Cup

Latasha Daneille, a poet and prose writer, is a free-spirited and fierce storyteller from Brooklyn, New York, whose voice illuminates the unvarnished human experience with the triumph of hope. Known for her incisive social commentary, she strategically uses multimedia platforms for creative expression. Her most recent works include the poetry mixtape "A Piece of Mind," the innovative CD-styled poetry book, *Pandemonium: Poems from a Pandemic*, and the acclaimed animated video, "Brooklyn Strong." Her debut short film, *Retrospection: A Look in the Mirror*, is being shown in New York state women's prisons as part of a rehabilitative arts reentry program.

Empty Cup

A PERSONAL REFLECTION by Latasha Daneille

Trauma has a name. Mine is called unhealed childhood wounds that left scars of rejection, abandon- ment, and the misconception that I was unlovable, or that I deserved to be loved by a person who lacked the capacity to love me beyond the walls of their empti- ness.

It wasn't an immediate manifestation of hurt, pain, or grief, but an accumulation of lived experiences triggered by seemingly in-nocent turbulence. Yet, unlike Maria, Dorian, Sandy, or Katrina —those natural disasters that stole lives and changed others—in my storm, self was the only collateral damage in a man-made calamity.

A bitter rift exists between my father and me concerning my marriage. And there's a cloud of tension that hovers heavily when we speak, so much so, little me considers, *maybe I owe him an apology*. Indeed, I robbed him of the opportunity to walk me down the aisle with a wide grin and a sense of pride and accomplishment that boasted of the hand he played in creating me. But do I? He stole my youth. I was never daddy's little girl. I was born at 16, the year that normally a young girl transitions to young adulthood with the firm hand of a father and the stern tongue of a mother warning, "Don't give away the milk for free."

Instead, I was left to figure out who I was and how a man was supposed to treat me. To sit on another man's knee and hope he would love and see me for who I was or could become. I searched for a paternal presence to call me princess and shower me with compliments and fancy things simply because he loved me. My fa-ther never married my 15-year-old mother. He drank the milk and left her with the burden and responsibility of raising a child while he roamed free. So, I have no regrets that he was absent on my wedding day since he was never present for my entire life. In fact, I blame him. I married a man just like my father, and he left me, too. But when my husband left, I died. And a vulnerable child was reborn, bruised, battered, and struggling to breathe, aching for someone to hear my infantile cries and say, "It's okay baby, Daddy's here." No. I don't owe my father an apology. He owes me.

"You don't understand, I keep telling you I have insomnia. I can't sleep," my father whined in his gravelly voice on the other end of the phone line. I rolled my eyes as I stood in the center of my brightly lit kitchen, gripping the cordless phone with disgust.

"Yes, you keep saying that. So, why can't you sleep? What's stopping you?"

I'm sure I sounded disinterested. I was. But I am also sure my father was oblivious to my lackadaisical concern. As long as I heard him, it didn't matter if he heard me. His labored breathing filled the pregnant pause on the call. I searched the silence and found his sobs.

"I did things when I was younger that haunt me. When I close my eyes, I see their faces." "Well, you can't change what happened or what you did," said my voice of reason. I wasn't prepared for the unexpected rage, the wail of a wounded dog struck by a speeding car and left to die in the middle of the road…forgotten.

"YOU DON'T KNOW WHAT I DID!"

" I don't need to know. God knows. Give it to Him and go to sleep."

Different day. Same kitchen. Yet this time, my voice was gentle, soft, and soothing like Jergens Ultra Healing lotion. Its tone caressed the insecurities masked with callousness that my husband learned after 27 years of prison.

"I'm not going to spend the rest of my life thinking about what I did over 20 years ago," he argued with pride, not the type mustered from a sense of accomplishment, but the pride driven by a self-centered existence and inflated ego. My husband tried to convince me that he was nothing like my father, who also spent years in and out of prison. A part of me wanted to believe him. But since being released on parole, it became clear that he was more like him than I had ever realized.

Both were charming and likable men who dressed well, were born in August, shared the same first three digits of their social security number, loved their women, and their bottle. The latter is a lethal combination. Too much liquor around a woman who had too much of a man's abuse leads to high levels of reciprocal toxicity, whirlwind disputes, and climactic encounters that escalate to physical touch less than loving.

His body was tense, hard, and fixed. I couldn't move him, and I couldn't move towards him. There was an unfamiliar look in his eye, and even though mine were filled with tears and I pleaded with him to stay, I had no choice but to step aside and let the man I married leave. Leave so the anger could subside, and pray that the twinkle in his eye would return without the black void that stared straight through me to divide us. In hopes of a Hail Mary, I grabbed his arm in desperation. He was determined to go. I didn't know where he was going, and it seemed he didn't know either, but his tone of voice and choice of words were intentional.

"You only respond to violence," he roared.

Bewildered, I responded.

"No, I don't, and you are not violent."

At that point, I released my husband. I couldn't compete with his anger or his strength. Defeated, I gave up.

Our phone conversations had become intermittent. The distance was long, not just in the call, but with the love and affection connecting a married couple. When he called, my heart hung in the balance, waiting for him to say something that would heal the hurt. He never did. Even still, I'd answer when he rang. And when my fingers defied logic and dialed his number, he picked up.

"What's good?" I asked him after the first ring.

"You tell me," my ex-husband replied defensively.

" It's a greeting." Bored now with the games.

"Trying," was his dry response.

I sighed with relief after the call ended. I am no longer trying or have to try to please anyone. I pleasure myself.

My trauma has been renamed like the prisoner who is no longer called by a state-identified number or a wife who decides to leave, reclaim her identity, and give birth to a new she, her, me, who commands a seat at the table.

When I was born and the doctor announced it's a girl, my young mother said, "Put her back, she's not done yet." I am fully cooked now, my belly rests proudly on my lap. I've released the desire to be a stick figure— a one-dimensional entity that fits into anything. Now, I am a full-figured universe, consuming the life that I created within my womb beyond my mother's birth canal and throughout tunnels of disappointment.

In the kitchen, conversation meets at the intersection of consequences. Early in the morning, just before the sun would rise fully, my grandfather and I would sit at the wooden drop-leaf table and stare into the backyard. Our sight was slightly glazed by the morning dew that fogged the sliding glass door. Yet we would ruminate about our past dreams that never came to fruition and the future plans we dreamed of manifesting.

Now, as I sit at the kitchen table sipping my third cup of coffee, I inhale the swirling steam and breathe. This is what self-love feels like. The warmth of my ceramic mug brings me comfort, and the heat of the liquid java tingling my tongue and sliding down my throat, encourages me to confess out loud... "I am full."

I Come From Women Who Could Not Be Broken

Mary Ayorinde is a Nigerian writer and poet, whose work explores identity, memory, love, and becoming. Her work spans poetry and fiction, blending vivid expression with emotional depth. With a voice that is both lyrical and soul-deep, she crafts narratives that honor ancestral strength and emotional truth. She holds a degree in Mass Communication and is the creator of Mary's Musings, a Substack where she shares her writing and creative reflections.

I Come From Women Who Could Not Be Broken

A HYBRID WORK by Mary Ayorinde

I come from women who could not be broken,
whose backs bent like river reeds

but never snapped.
From women who sang while they scrubbed floors,
who braided resistance into cornrows,
who wore grief like gold,
and still danced
with smoke in their throats
and freedom in their feet.
I come from lullabies hummed in languages
the colonizer could not translate.
From wrists that stirred pots and revolutions
at the same time.
From grandmothers who knew how to stitch joy
into torn cloth,
who prayed not with words,
but with the way they stood tall
even when the world tried to cut them down.
I am the memory they buried
and the prophecy they whispered.
I am every "no" turned into a poem.
Every "you can't" rewritten
into a gospel of "watch me rise."
My story is not neat.
It is not soft.
It is not meant to be palatable.
It is carved in the rhythm of drums
that echo through my bones.
It is painted in the keloids of survival,
in the beauty of loud laughter
after generations of silence.
I come from Lagos rainstorms
and Sunday rice,

from thunder that knows my name
and ancestors who walk ahead of me
clearing paths I cannot see.
I write because I must.
Because if I don't,
the words will riot inside me—
they will turn my body into a battlefield
until every untold story finds breath.
This is not just poetry.
This is reclamation.
This is my voice,
uninterrupted.
This is me saying:
I was here.
I am here.
I will be here—
long after the page forgets my name
but remembers my fire.
So I write for the ones
who had no pen.
For the ones who swallowed their truth
so their children could eat.
For the ones who were told to shrink,
and instead, expanded into galaxies.
I come from women who could not be broken—
and I am proof
they never were.

my house of stone.

Namatayi Omolara Mavunga is a Zimbabwean-Nigerian writer and actor based in London. A recent First class honours graduate from the University of Essex, Namatayi draws on the richness of their heritage to explore themes of diaspora, belonging, and identity. Their work reflects the ache of ancestral longing, the joy of unexpected community, and the beautifully complex experience of being a Black African lesbian. Namatayi writes across various forms: scripts, poetry, short fiction, and book reviews - and shares her work on Substack as @fromspringwithlove and on Instagram at @namatayislibrary.

my house of stone.

A POEM by Namatayi Mavunga

to celebrate an independence day is to
acknowledge the death of your country / happy birthday zimbabwe 45 years of being /

liberated / free? / returned / all synonyms of independent /
but what are you talking about? /
the blood on the walls is scarlet / and the blood is yours / the
chains on his feet are not
invisible / i met a white south african who called me rhode-
sian and i felt / sick to my stomach
with the direction zimbabwe is going / did you know we /
used to be the breadbasket of africa
/ do you know why
wait — what? why?
they used the zimbabwean body for cheap labour and profited
off our broken bones, you
know how the story goes.
I didn't.
well. they destroyed everything we called ours / and they
never let us talk about it / that's on
purpose / the system is in place so we never see who's pulling
our strings / distract distract
distract / cecil john rhodes / ~~don't mention him on indepen-~~
~~dence day~~ / white hands never left
black necks / don't / look up / can't / look up.
to celebrate an independence day is to
feel pride.
(there is ash in my mouth because something is burning)
feel pride.
(the smoke rises, and everything is on fire)
feel pride.
(my grandad sends all of his money back home, and still it is
not enough)
feel pride.

(can my ancestors hear me? can they hear us over all of this
noise?)
feel pride.
(can you hear me over all of this noise?
feel pride.
(what is there to be proud about?)
feel pride.
(everything. resilience is in our bones we rise like our golden
eagle and fly again.)
feel pride.
(my words ring flat and off-key against my ears.)
the mbira in my hand connects me to a spirit like a phone op-
erator.
hello this is the ancestral plane of southern africa, your sur-
name and country of birth please.
if only.
I imagine, as I always do when my hands run over the keys,
my ancestors. i imagine them
together watching me thinking this child doesn't know what
they're doing. the child born to
the diaspora clings to whatever pieces of their history exist,
their culture. i don't know if it's
disappointment or curiosity that dances across their faces. per-
haps it is one of the same. in
my minds' eye, there- just slightly separated from the rest, is a
woman. she looks. so similar
to me, black skin, soft eyes and a full mouth which stretches to
a smile, you'll learn she
whispers.
happy independence day zimbabwe. my house of stone. may
the land be greener than

yesterday. lush and full of life. may the blood that once soaked
be a reminder for all we have
lost, and a warning for all that we continue to. may the gold
return under the darkness of
spring,
and may the zimbabwean people look up, look up, look up.

FREEDOM!!!

I am not free while any woman is unfree

Enza M. (she/her) is a 19-year-old writer and Political Science student at the University of Amsterdam. Her work moves through womanhood, rage, beauty, culture and survival—often in the same breath. Blending poetry, essays, and a touch of rebellion, she writes to question everything we've been told to accept. Her pieces live on *4nzza*, her Substack, where a growing audience returns for her down to earth and soul speaking pieces.

I am not free while any woman is unfree

A HYBRID WORK by Enza Mugabkazi

Content Warning:

This piece contains descriptions of gender-based violence including breast ironing, female genital mutilation, child marriage, war-related trauma and emotional distress. Reader discretion is advised.

She was ten when her mother started ironing her chest.

She thought it was just warmth at first, a strange kind of mother's touch. Until the pestle, pulled from the fire, kissed her budding breasts and her skin peeled like bark from a tree. Every morning, before the sun could bear witness, her mother would press it down again. Again and again. Praying that if the breasts didn't grow, the men wouldn't come. That if she looked like a child, she'd be spared from becoming a bride.

But they came anyway.

Another girl, across mountains, sewn shut between her legs, because they told her pain is purity. Told her the blood that gushes from her when she walks is better than the pleasure she might feel if they left her whole. They told her she'd be a wife now, even if she still played with dolls. They told her it's tradition. That her scream was part of becoming a woman.

And I? I am supposed to write pretty words about *freedom*?

I can't. I won't. I'm not free. I'm not free and I won't pretend to be while my sisters are being butchered in the name of culture, buried under bombs, or forced to smile through shattered teeth.

I'm not free if I still smell blood in Sudan, in Palestine, in Congo — where girls hold their dolls tighter than their mothers because sometimes, only one of them comes back from the rubble.

I am not free because every woman I meet has a story. A story where they felt robbed of their humanness, where they felt *betrayed* by God.

How do I dare to breathe like freedom while others are suffocating? How do I dare to write if a girl somewhere doesn't even know what letters are? What is a voice to me if my sisters are forbidden to speak?

I'm tired.

Tired of seeing girls turned into wives before they even understand their own names.

Tired of being told we are too loud, too soft, too angry, too emotional, too "too".

Tired of watching women be strong because no one ever let them be safe.

I am haunted by every woman I've never met,
the ones who walk with *ashes* in their throats,
the ones who carry dead babies on their backs and still keep walking,
the ones who wipe their tears with hands that are still washing dishes for their ungrateful husbands,
the ones who never got the chance to become anything but someone's daughter, someone's wife, someone's *possession.*

We are hunted, haunted, handled, hidden.
And still, we rise.

I am a woman, and that alone makes the earth tremble.

But being a woman also means I have learned how to carry pain like perfume. How to take rage and make it beautiful. How to bleed and bloom all at once. I am angry, yes, but I cry too. I cry for the girls who don't know why they're hurting. I cry for the women who think pain is love. I cry for all of us who were taught to fold our power into apology.

But I will no longer be silent. Silence is betrayal now.

So this is what I'll do.

I will write.

I will fight.

I will carry their names on my back like ancestral prayers, whispered through clenched teeth.

I will be the voice for the girl who never got to speak, the one whose silence wasn't a choice but a sentence.

I will make sure she is heard, even if the world has already forgotten her.

Because it's in my bones now,
this grief, this fury, this love.
It runs through me like blood.
I do not carry these women's stories out of charity, I carry them because they are etched into the deepest part of me.
Because when one girl is mutilated, I flinch.
When one woman is beaten, I ache.
When another is buried too soon, a part of me dies with her.

This has never just been about me.
It's about all of us.
The ones still here.
The ones who never made it out.
The ones just now opening their eyes to the cage around them.

We are not free but we are awakening.
And from that awakening will come something terrifying and tender.
A movement not born in noise, but in knowing.
Not sudden, but unstoppable.

It hasn't started with me.
But it continues through me —
And when I am gone, I will have left behind pages soaked in truth,
And daughters who do not ask for permission.
And that?
That will be enough.

Des Pres

A Friend Asked Me "What Sinners (2025) ...

Johnna Parker (she/her) is a Black femme poet/writer from North Carolina. She is a senior in college studying English and creative writing. Her work has appeared in HOMIES, Afro Poetist, The Faoileánach Journal, and Opal Age Tribune. You can find her on Instagram @ _johnna.nicole_ and on Substack @ anxiousblkgirl.

A Friend Asked Me "What Sinners (2025) Was Even About" and I've Been Waiting to Write This Poem for a Long Time

A POEM by Johnna Parker

nina simone said "the people that built their heaven

on your land are telling you yours is in the sky."

and all my life i've been told that what lies down here is no par-
adise for us Black folk,

we just survive long enough to say we lived right enough to make
it to a promised land.

so, for a few hours we make our own on this here ground: in aban-
doned barns

and forbidden houses. with the pardoning of the sun comes a joy
unimaginable, and we radiate it

from our deep-pearled skin. under warm lamplight we dance with
country dirt beneath our feet—

sway, two-step, and gyrate. with our bodies we call upon a lineage

of joy amidst the struggle to conjure

a life worth living. with heads tilted and shoulders high we rejoice
in song and stomp; moan,

eyes closed, molten morsels melting in our mouths; make love in
private corners not thinking

about the morning—not thinking about the inevitable devil, on
his way as we speak, waiting for

the sun to rise. we pay no mind to the teachings of hellish land and
holy sky, making a small

heaven on our very own Black earth, for a night.

Black is beautiful
Black is beautiful
Black is beautiful, Black is beautiful, Black is
black
DesPres

6-Pack of Pepsi

Dr. Gloria Renee Bland is a poet, creative writer, preacher, teacher, wife, mother, and grammy who looks for inspiration in a drop of water or grain of rice. She is a graduate of Pittsburgh Theological Seminary with a Doctorate in Creative Writing and Public Theology. She lives by daily asking herself and others, "What brings you joy?"

6-Pack of Pepsi

A POEM by Dr. Gloria Renee Bland

Lorraine! Walk up the street to the store and bring Mama Grace back a six-pack of
Pepsi.
My name is not Lorraine. I do have a cousin named Lorraine. We don't look like each other
though we are both beautiful black women. And we're both ordained clergy.
Perhaps she was looking at our spirits when she said to me,

Lorraine! Walk up the street to the store and bring Mama Grace back a six-pack of

Pepsi.

My mama fusses at her mama, whom she calls

Mums!

You know that child's name is not Lorraine! MY daughter's name is Renee!

Mother turns to daughter and says,

She knows what her name is.

Mama Grace, Cause she is too GRAND to be called a grand-mother, turns to me and

says,

You know what your name is don't you?

Yes ma'am, I do.

Mother turns to daughter with a big satisfying smirk on face and a nod.

She turns back to me and says,

Lorraine! Walk up the street to the store and bring Mama Grace back a six-pack of

Pepsi.

I quickly walk out the door, leaving mother and daughter in a standoff. $20 bill in hand, I

walk to the store to get the six-pack of Pepsi.

Pepsi's becomes a running joke among the cousins. Whether it is the fountain-poured

Small Pepsi from the People's Drug Store lunch counter, where we would would secure

Mama Grace a beef-barbeque burger with plain chips to go along with her Pepsi, or the

golden arches where we knew her standard order, one hamburger happy meal with a

Pepsi, we find the whole thing rather comical. It is especially funny when we have to go

through the drive-thru at the golden arches and whisper the word for the other

carbonated brown beverage because Mama Grace did not want no parts of the other.

EVER!

Except when attending gatherings where people did not understand she only drinks

Pepsi and instead had the alternative brown elixir, then we had to tell her it was...

Lorraine! Walk up the street to the store and bring Mama Grace back a six-pack of

Pepsi.

Every now and then she let me have one of her unopened Pepsi's. Otherwise, she

offers one that was sitting in the refrigerator for two or three days, partially empty from

being used for her lunch or dinner meals which must include her Pepsi.

You cannot say no to the flat, unappetizing liquid because it is Mama Grace and you do

not say no to Mama Grace.

I did not understand why it has to be Pepsi and why she had to have it every day

until

I

understood.

Pepsi is this prim proper look down her nose upper middle class elite THE songbird of

Texas pink lipstick dress and heels wearing raised her seven children a block away from

Howard University on Harvard Street with her husband the honored military officer

preacher Truant Officer for the Color School System in Washington, D.C. whose

children went to Dunbar High School and Cardozo High School and Minor Teachers

College.

This woman shows her stand against oppression and suppression and segregation and

Jim Crow and racial discrimination and women discrimination and,

and,

and,

One Pepsi at a time, she reminds herself Coke did not want no parts of the Negroes in

America and blatantly marketed to the whites back-in-the-day.

Pepsi went after the Negro market and won the battle if not the war.

And my GRANDmother, Grace Darling Young Johnson stood on the side of right and

righteousness one Pepsi at a time.

Renee! Walk up the street to the store and bring Mama Grace back a six-pack of Pepsi.

And unbeknownst to this GRANDdaughter with each step, I too, walk and move on the

side of right and righteousness

11

11

11

Pepsi at a time

About the Editors

Desiree McCray (she/they) offers the literary canon a Black theo-poetic voice that bridges prayer, protest, and prophetic imagination, reimagining the sacred as present within the everyday realities of Black women's lives. McCray founded DJELI which stands for **Diversity, Justice, and Equity for Literary Impact,** in 2024. As the Editor-in-Chief of *DJELI JOURNAL,* they are excited to bring Black women and nonbinary people's stories to the page. Drawing on womanist theology, McCray writes with a lyricism that is both spiritual and subversive, transforming poetry into a liturgical space where lament, joy, and embodiment coexist. Her work—spanning collections titled *Hope Among Other Foods, Send A Refreshing, My Sisters Look Like God,* and *Black Girl, Brown Soul*—pushes beyond traditional boundaries of genre, blending sermon, song, and personal testimony into a poetics of liberation. In the spirit of Audre Lorde and Lucille Clifton, McCray claims the margins as holy ground, where fat joy, ancestral memory, and radical care reveal divine truth. By fusing theology and literature, she expands the canon's spiritual imagination, offering a voice that calls both readers and institutions to reckon with a faith that is unapologetically embodied, communal, and revolutionary.

Kyron "Spirit" Elam has spent his entire life writing a myriad of poems, short stories, and songs. As Deputy Editor of *DJELI JOURNAL*, he has sat with the stories and poems of this collection and helped shape it into something cohesive. Kyron graduated from the University of Missouri in 2018 with a B.A. in Interdisciplinary Studies and a Multicultural Certificate. Since then, he has completed two Master's from both Mizzou and DePaul University in the field of education while expanding his writing portfolio to the role of editing. He currently works to support the minds of the future, particularly the multilingual learners, as a high school Bilingual English teacher while maintaining his writing career. *Shades of a Love-a-holic* is his first published work. In his free time, he enjoys anime, games and other media, studying languages and other texts, and exploring new flavors whether eating or cooking with his son and fiancée.